9-06

P9-EDY-350

THE SOLAR SYSTEM

VENUS

A MyReportLinks.com Book

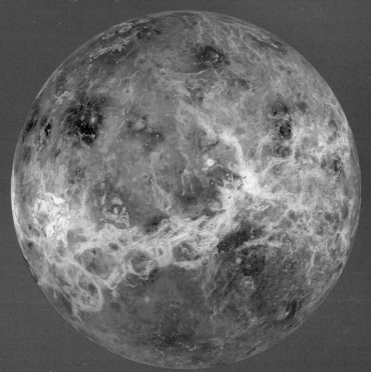

STEPHEN FEINSTEIN

MyReportLinks.com Books

an imprint of

 Enslow Publishers, Inc.

Box 398, 40 Industrial Road
Berkeley Heights, NJ 07922
USA

MyReportLinks.com Books, an imprint of Enslow Publishers, Inc. MyReportLinks® is a registered trademark of Enslow Publishers, Inc.

Library of Congress Cataloging-in-Publication Data

Feinstein, Stephen.
  Venus / Stephen Feinstein.
    p. cm. — (The solar system)
  Includes bibliographical references and index.
  ISBN 0-7660-5300-8
  1. Venus (Planet)—Juvenile literature. I. Title. II. Solar system (Berkeley Heights, N.J.)
  QB621.F45 2005
  523.42—dc22

                                  2004008286

Printed in the United States of America

10 9 8 7 6 5 4 3 2 1

To Our Readers:
Through the purchase of this book, you and your library gain access to the Report Links that specifically back up this book.
The Publisher will provide access to the Report Links that back up this book and will keep these Report Links up to date on **www.myreportlinks.com** for five years from the book's first publication date.
We have done our best to make sure all Internet addresses in this book were active and appropriate when we went to press. However, the author and the Publisher have no control over, and assume no liability for, the material available on those Internet sites or on other Web sites they may link to.
The usage of the MyReportLinks.com Books Web site is subject to the terms and conditions stated on the Usage Policy Statement on **www.myreportlinks.com**.
A password may be required to access the Report Links that back up this book. The password is found on the bottom of page 4 of this book.
Any comments or suggestions can be sent by e-mail to comments@myreportlinks.com or to the address on the back cover.

Photo Credits: © Corel Corporation, pp. 14, 15; Clipart.com, pp. 9, 16; Enslow Publishers, Inc., p. 28; European Southern Observatory, p. 34; Library of Congress, p. 18; Michael Wilce/European Southern Observatory, p. 29; MyReportLinks.com Books, p. 4; National Aeronautics and Space Administration (NASA), pp. 1, 3, 9, 11, 13, 20, 21, 22, 24, 25, 31, 33, 35, 37, 38, 40, 43, 44; Nine Planets, p. 10; Photos.com, p. 3; Smithsonian Institution, p. 17; Venus Transit, p. 36.

Cover Photo: National Aeronautics and Space Administration.

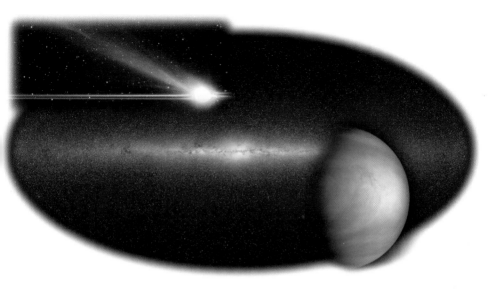

Back	Forward	Stop	Review	Home	Explore	Favorites	History

About MyReportLinks.com Books

MyReportLinks.com Books
Great Books, Great Links, Great for Research!

The Internet sites listed on the next four pages can save you hours of research time. These Internet sites—we call them "Report Links"—are constantly changing, but we keep them up to date on our Web site.

Give it a try! Type http://www.myreportlinks.com into your browser, click on the series title, then the book title, and scroll down to the Report Links listed for this book.

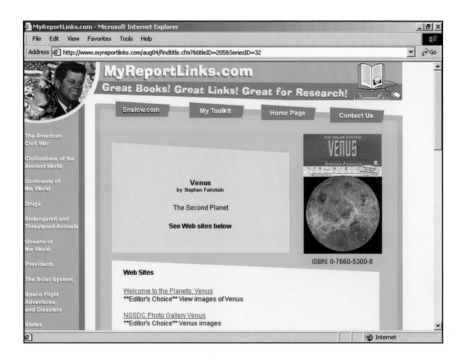

The Report Links will bring you to great source documents, photographs, and illustrations. MyReportLinks.com Books save you time, feature Report Links that are kept up to date, and make report writing easier than ever!

Please see "To Our Readers" on the copyright page for important information about this book, the MyReportLinks.com Web site, and the Report Links that back up this book.

Please enter **PVE1610** if asked for a password.

Report Links

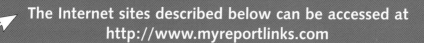
The Internet sites described below can be accessed at
http://www.myreportlinks.com

*EDITOR'S CHOICE

▶Welcome to the Planets: Venus
On this NASA Web site, you can view images of Venus. The images
come with a zoom feature and descriptions. Terms are explained in
a glossary.

*EDITOR'S CHOICE

▶NSSDC Photo Gallery Venus
This site includes thumbnails of the best photos of Venus, a description
of each one, and a link to view and download high-resolution photos
that can be used to illustrate reports.

*EDITOR'S CHOICE

▶Venus
This is a nice summary of the properties and features of Venus with
photo illustrations. Read a story about why some astronomers thought
Venus had a moon named Neith.

*EDITOR'S CHOICE

▶Astronomy—Venus
What we have learned about Venus through space missions is profiled
chronologically in this NASA site.

*EDITOR'S CHOICE

▶Astronomy for Kids—Venus
This site designed for kids offers an interesting look at Venus, including
a history of mythology concerning the planet, a description of its
atmosphere, and a word-search puzzle. Click on the sky map to find
out where Venus is located.

*EDITOR'S CHOICE

▶Venus: Adler Planetarium
This site includes pictures and descriptions of spacecraft that have
collected information about Venus, an interactive map, and answers
to commonly asked questions about Earth's "twin planet."

		STOP					
Back	Forward	Stop	Review	Home	Explore	Favorites	History

Report Links

The Internet sites described below can be accessed at http://www.myreportlinks.com

▶**Astronomy Dictionary**

Terms used in astronomy and their definitions have been compiled and written for kids in this easy-to-use online dictionary.

▶**BBC History: Jeremiah Horrocks**

This BBC site offers a brief biography of Jeremiah Horrocks, a seventeenth-century English astronomer who was the first person to accurately predict and see a transit of Venus.

▶**Chasing Venus: Observing the Transits of Venus**

Archival images and detailed historical accounts from the Smithsonian Institution Libraries explore the history of astronomers who "chased Venus" in their attempts to witness the planet's alignment with the Sun and Earth.

▶**Chronology of Venus Exploration**

This time line lists the spacecraft that have successfully and unsuccessfully attempted missions to Venus, from *Sputnik 7* in 1961 to the present. It also includes descriptions of missions planned for the future.

▶**European Southern Observatory**

This Web site contains fascinating photographs from around the world of Venus's June 8, 2004, transit of the Sun. (If you missed your opportunity to see it then, you will have another chance in 2012.)

▶**Exploring the Planets: Venus**

This Web site from the Smithsonian Institution's National Air and Space Museum provides basic facts about Venus as well as information on the *Magellan* mission.

▶**Global Warming Kids Site**

Global warming and the greenhouse effect on Earth are explained in this site for kids from the federal government's Environmental Protection Agency. It also includes games and animations.

▶**Global Warming Time Line**

View a time line of changes in Earth's climate from 1800 to 1988 that are related to global warming, and read about the discovery of global warming on Venus. Links to detailed articles are included.

Any comments? Contact us: **comments@myreportlinks.com**

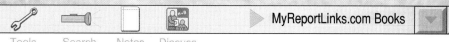
Report Links

The Internet sites described below can be accessed at http://www.myreportlinks.com

▶**The *Magellan* Spacecraft at Venus**

Where is Venus? How does *Magellan* take pictures of this planet through its clouds? How does Venus's surface compare with Earth's? The answers to these and other questions are found in this site.

▶**Mayan Astronomy**

The site describes the astronomical achievements of the Maya, who accurately tracked Venus thousands of years ago.

▶**MYSTARSLIVE.COM**

Where is Venus now? At this site, enter your location and pick a time and direction (Venus will be in the western or eastern horizon charts). The program creates a star chart showing the locations of planets and constellations.

▶**National Weather Service—Venus**

This site from the National Weather Service offers a brief look at the atmosphere and weather of Venus.

▶**Pictures of Venus Crossing the Sun**

This Space.com Web page offers images from around the world of the June 8, 2004, transit of Venus. Reactions from spectators of this most recent event and a history of Venus's transits are also included.

▶**The Planet Venus**

This site provides lots of facts about Venus, including descriptions of its surface features, cloud layers, and more.

▶**Time Line**

A time line of astronomical discovery, spanning more than five thousand years, is featured in this site. Click on "Forward" at the bottom of the page to view more modern achievements.

▶**2004 and 2012 Transits of Venus**

What is a transit of Venus? This site explains that phenomenon and offers a chart to illustrate its components. Check out the maps to see if you live in an area where the next transit—in June 2012—will be visible.

Report Links

The Internet sites described below can be accessed at http://www.myreportlinks.com

▶**Venus Nomenclature Table of Contents**

On this site, you can click on the name of a feature found on Venus, such as "regio" or "vallis" and find background information about that feature.

▶**USGS Astrogeology Research Program: Venus 1:10 Million-Scale Quads**

Labeled surface maps of Venus are the highlight of this Web site. Click on a section and get a color map of that area with its features labeled.

▶**Venus: The Fire-drenched Goddess**

Data on Venus's atmosphere, magnetic field, surface features, and interior are included in this site.

▶**Venus Picture List**

This extensive collection of online images of Venus includes images taken from Russian and American spacecraft.

▶**Venus—Enchanted Learning**

An introduction to Venus is offered at this Web site, which also includes links to a page that provides tips for writing reports about the planets.

▶**Views of the Solar System**

On this site from Solarviews, you can find information about Venus, the Sun, the Moon, and other interesting topics related to space and astronomy.

▶**Welcome to the Planets**

This NASA site presents an overview of the planets in our solar system and includes a gallery of images.

▶**Windows to the Universe: Venus**

This Web site provides a basic overview of Venus. Information on the atmosphere, interior, surface, space missions, and more is included.

Any comments? Contact us: **comments@myreportlinks.com**

Venus Facts

Age
About 4.5 billion years

Diameter
7,521 miles (12,104 kilometers)

Composition
Molten metal core; mantle and crust of various rock

Distance From the Sun
About 67 million miles (108 million kilometers)

Closest Approach to Earth
24 million miles (38 million kilometers)

Orbital Period (year, in Earth days)
225 Earth days

Rotational Period (day, in Earth days)
243 Earth days

Mass
82 percent of Earth's mass

Temperature
900°F (482°C) at surface

Surface Gravity
91 percent of Earth's gravity

Chapter 1 ▶

Earth's Twin Planet

Venus, the second planet from the Sun in the solar system, has long been considered Earth's twin planet. It is closer to Earth than any other planet, about 23.7 million miles (38.1 million kilometers) away at its closest. Both planets were formed about 4.5 billion years ago. Both planets are solid rocky objects with atmospheres, and they have similar densities and compositions. Venus is roughly

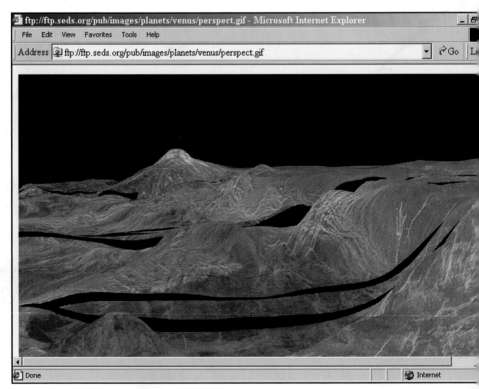

ftp://ftp.seds.org/pub/images/planets/venus/perspect.gif - Microsoft Internet Explorer

File   Edit   View   Favorites   Tools   Help

Address ftp://ftp.seds.org/pub/images/planets/venus/perspect.gif   ⏣ Go

Done   Internet

▲ The Lakshmi Plateau is located in a large highland region of Venus known as Ishtar Terra. This rolling plateau is named for the Hindu goddess of wealth and good fortune.

▲ *Venus (top) and Earth are similar in size, which is why Venus was called Earth's twin planet for centuries. Scientists now know that the second planet from the Sun is very different from our own.*

the same size as Earth, although slightly smaller, with a diameter at its equator of about 7,521 miles (12,104 kilometers).

But unlike Earth, whose satellite is the Moon, Venus has no natural satellite. And unlike Earth, you will not find any human beings living on Venus—and it is doubtful, though not impossible, that other forms of life exist there.

Rolling Plains and Highlands

Most of Venus's surface consists of rolling plains, but there are also three large highland, or "continental," areas—Ishtar Terra, Aphrodite Terra, and Beta Regio. Ishtar Terra is larger than the continental United States. The Lakshmi Plateau is located in Ishtar Terra, as is the seven-mile-high (eleven-kilometer-high) Maxwell Montes, the highest mountain on Venus. Maxwell Montes is a mile higher than Mount Everest, the highest mountain on Earth.

Aphrodite Terra, the largest of the highland regions, is about the same size as South America. Near Venus's equator, in Aphrodite Terra, is the huge volcano Maat Mons. Lava flows surround the volcano, and scientists estimate that these flows were no more than ten years old when they were first observed by the space probe *Magellan* in 1990. This has led scientists to conclude that volcanic action is still taking place on Venus.[1]

Venus is the brightest object in the night sky, except for the Sun and the Moon. It is far brighter than any star seen from Earth. Venus's brightness is caused by sunlight reflecting off the thick layer of clouds that blankets the planet. Because of its dazzling brightness, Venus has had a powerful influence on the beliefs of ancient cultures and civilizations, inspiring worship and wonder.

The Morning Star and the Evening Star

Thousands of years ago, most people had very different ideas about the heavens than we do today. For example, many believed that Earth was flat and that all heavenly bodies moved around Earth.

This hemispheric view of Venus was taken by cameras aboard NASA's Magellan *spacecraft. Launched in 1989,* Magellan *reached Venus a year later and made more than fifteen thousand orbits of the planet.*

They assumed that the planets were either gods or goddesses, believing that the Sun made a journey across the sky each day and then spent each night in the Underworld. Ancient astronomers did not understand the motions of the planets as we do today, especially the apparent complex motions of Venus. They did not understand that Venus's orbital motion causes it to appear in different parts of the sky at different times. Therefore, many people in the ancient world believed that Venus was actually two different bodies—the morning star and the evening star.

Since Venus is closer to the Sun than we are, we cannot see Venus when we are facing away from the Sun. So Venus is not visible in the middle of the night. However, Venus is visible in

▲ *Ancient astronomers named the planet Venus after the Roman goddess of love and beauty. This statue of the goddess is one of the most famous figures in western art.*

the morning sky in the east for about nine months at a time. At other times, Venus is visible in the evening sky in the west. The ancient Egyptians had two names for the planet: Ouaiti, the evening star, and Tioumoutiri, the morning star. The early Greeks called the morning star Phosphoros, or "light bearer," and the evening star Hesperos, or "west."

▷ The Planet of Love and Beauty

Not all ancient people, however, believed in "two Venuses." The Babylonians, who were among the earliest astronomers, concluded that the morning and evening stars were actually one and the same. They called this star Ishtar, "the bright torch of heaven," after their most widely worshiped goddess. She was the embodiment of woman and the mother of the gods, and she was also the goddess of war. The Babylonian Venus Tablet, which was written between 1646 B.C. and 1626 B.C., is the earliest recorded observation of Venus that has come down to us.[2] Later, Pythagoras, who was a sixth-century B.C. Greek philosopher, mathematician, and astronomer, also realized that the morning and evening stars were the same star. The Greeks then named this star after Aphrodite, their goddess of love and beauty. The Romans named it Venus, their name for the same goddess, which is the name we still use today for the planet.

Not every ancient culture associated the planet Venus with feminine qualities. To the Aztecs, in Mexico, Venus as the morning star represented Tlahuizcalpantecuhtli, "Lord of the House of Dawn." The planet was a manifestation of Quetzalcoatl, a god associated with the wind and air and identified by a feathered serpent.

The Maya Temple of Kukulcán at Chichén Itzá. Maya astronomers created amazingly accurate calendars based on their observations of the planet Venus and other celestial bodies.

In 1610, the Italian scientist Galileo Galilei was the first person to observe Venus's phases. He was able to do this through a telescope he made that was far more powerful than earlier instruments.

Another ancient culture from Mesoamerica called the Maya considered Venus to be a representation of Kukulcán, their name for Quetzalcoatl. The Maya carefully observed the movements of Venus and accurately calculated the cycle in which Venus would repeat its movement in relation to the Sun. They created a calendar based on this 260-day cycle. The Maya also believed that life on Earth would not exist without Venus. Maya astronomer-priests showed their gratitude to the planet through offerings that included human sacrifice. For the Maya, Venus played an important role in the unfolding of historical events. At Bonampak, a Maya city in what is today southern Mexico, the priests of the Maya king Chaan-Muan kept secret Venus tables to predict important astronomical events and used Venus's appearances to plan battles.

Venus and the Birth of Modern Astronomy

During the Renaissance, the period in Europe from the four-teenth through the seventeenth centuries that marked the beginnings of modern science, our understanding of the solar system and its planets took a great leap forward. In 1543, the Polish astronomer Nicolaus Copernicus published his theory that Earth and all the other planets revolved around the Sun. Copernicus' theory, known as the heliocentric theory, challenged Ptolemy's geocentric theory. Ptolemy, a Greek astronomer of the second century A.D., believed that all the heavenly bodies revolved around Earth, and that belief was commonly held for more than a thousand years.

In 1610, Galileo Galilei, an Italian astronomer and physicist who agreed with Copernicus' theory, became the first astronomer to observe Venus through a telescope. He noticed that Venus had changing phases, like the Moon. This convinced him that Venus

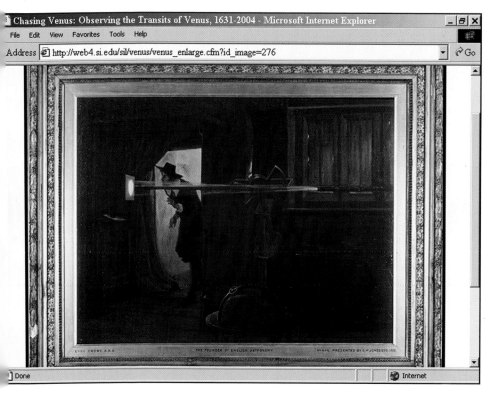

Chasing Venus: Observing the Transits of Venus, 1631-2004 - Microsoft Internet Explorer

File   Edit   View   Favorites   Tools   Help

Address 🖾 http://web4.si.edu/sil/venus/venus_enlarge.cfm?id_image=276   ℰ Go

△ *Painted 250 years after his death,* Jeremiah Horrocks Watching the Transit of Venus in 1639 *is a Victorian view of the pioneering seventeenth-century English astronomer. Horrocks was the first to predict and witness a transit of Venus.*

⏶ An engraving of Sir John Herschel's forty-foot telescope, which was enormous for its time.

revolved around the Sun. As it did so, there was always one side of the planet that was sunlit and one side in shadow. Galileo's observations of Venus and other planets supported Copernicus' heliocentric theory.

▷ The Transit of Venus

In 1639, an English astronomer named Jeremiah Horrocks became the first person to accurately predict and witness a transit of Venus, which occurs when Venus's path takes it directly between Earth and the Sun. When this happens, Venus can be seen as a little black circle moving across the face of the Sun.

Horrocks was also able to calculate Venus's size as well as the distance between Earth and the Sun more accurately than had ever been done before.

In 1761, Mikhail Lomonosov, a Russian scientist, observed a transit of Venus and noted that Venus's disk was fuzzy rather than sharp and had a halo around it. His observations led to the discovery that Venus has an atmosphere. In 1769, Captain James Cook, an English explorer and navigator, observed a transit of Venus from the island of Tahiti in the South Pacific. Calculations made from these observations enabled astronomers to work out relative measurements of the planets in the solar system.

In 1850, Sir John Herschel, an English astronomer, observed Venus and concluded that the planet's brightness was caused by cloud cover reflecting sunlight. He said of Venus, "We see clearly that its surface is not mottled over with permanent spots like the Moon; we notice in it neither mountains nor shadows, but a uniform brightness, in which sometimes we may indeed fancy, or perhaps more than fancy, brighter or obscurer portions, but can seldom or never rest fully satisfied of the fact."[3]

Beneath the Clouds of Venus

Once astronomers realized that Venus was covered by clouds, they began to wonder what lay beneath them. Since no telescope could penetrate the thick, yellowish clouds, the surface of Venus was veiled in mystery. Astronomers and other scientists were left imagining whether Venus might have intelligent life similar to

Windows to the Universe - Microsoft Internet Explorer

File   Edit   View   Favorites   Tools   Help

Address http://www.windows.ucar.edu/tour/link=/venus/images/global_image.html   Go   Link

Done   Internet

▲ *This global view of Venus's surface comes from radar images compiled by the* Magellan *mission. The colors, which have been added, are based on actual color photos taken by Soviet* Venera *spacecraft.*

Venus's surface at different latitudes is displayed in these five global images. They represent a composite of all the radar images collected during the Magellan mission.

that on Earth, since both planets seemed so much alike. In 1894, a French astronomer named Camille Flammarion wrote:

> Of what nature are the inhabitants of Venus? Are they endowed with intelligence analogous to our own? Do they resemble us in physical form? . . .These are interesting questions, to which we have no reply. All that we can say is, that organized life on Venus must

▲ *Venus's clouds of sulfuric acid were captured in this image taken nearly 2 million miles away from the planet during the Galileo mission. The picture is shown through a filter and has been tinted blue to emphasize the subtle changes in the cloud markings.*

be little different from terrestrial life [life on Earth], and that this world is one of those which resemble ours most.[1]

▶ A Warm, Wet World?

Scientists reasoned that because Venus is closer to the Sun than Earth is, Venus must be warmer than Earth. They also thought that Venus's ever-present cloud cover indicated the presence of water, so the planet must be warm and humid. Perhaps it rained there all the time. Some scientists believed that there were tropical jungles on Venus, possibly inhabited by dinosaurs and other exotic creatures. Others theorized that Venus was completely covered by an ocean. These theories continued until the mid- to late-twentieth century. It was not until the 1960s and 1970s, when the American *Mariner* and Soviet *Venera* spacecraft reached Venus, that the planet gave up some of its secrets. And Venus turned out to be totally different than anyone had expected.

A Dry, Hot, Poisonous World

We now know that although Venus does resemble Earth in certain ways, it is not a friendly, watery planet. Instead, it is dry, scorching hot, and poisonous—things not usually associated with a goddess of love and beauty. The famous author, astronomer, and educator Carl Sagan remarked about this in one of his books: "Venus seems less the goddess of love than the incarnation of hell."[2] Venus's extremely dense atmosphere consists of 96 percent carbon dioxide and 3 percent nitrogen, with trace amounts of sulfur dioxide, water vapor, and other gases. Air pressure at the surface is ninety-two times that of Earth, similar to the crushing pressure 3,000 feet (914 meters) below the surface of Earth's oceans.

Venus's clouds are formed by the Sun's ultraviolet rays reacting with chemicals in the planet's atmosphere. The clouds contain poisonous droplets of sulfuric acid. There are three main cloud layers in Venus's atmosphere. The upper cloud layer, at 45 miles (72 kilometers) above the planet's surface, is extremely cold, at −150°F (−101°C). The bottom layer of clouds, meanwhile, is oven-hot, at 400°F (204°C). Within these cloud layers, the air is hazy. The top layer of clouds whips around Venus at about two hundred miles per hour (three hundred kilometers per hour). At the surface, there is hardly any wind at all.

Venus's ever-present, thick cloud cover traps heat from the Sun, preventing it from radiating back into space, much like the glass in a greenhouse traps the Sun's rays. This results in what is

▲ *Maat Mons, the highest volcano on Venus, is named for an Egyptian goddess of truth and justice. (Maat is the name of the goddess; mons is Latin for "mount" or "mountain.")*

known as the greenhouse effect. The average temperature on the surface of Venus is nearly 900°F (482°C), hot enough to melt sulfur, lead, zinc, and tin—and your school desk. With such high temperatures, it is unlikely that humans will ever be able to set foot on the surface of Venus. So far, all exploration of Venus has been done by unmanned orbiting spacecraft and robotic landers.

Pancake Domes, Arachnoids, and Other Strange Features

What those craft have discovered is that Venus has more volcanoes and lava flows than any other planet in the solar system. Maat Mons, the highest volcano on Venus, rises for more than five miles (about eight kilometers) above the surrounding plains. It may have erupted as recently as fifty years ago. Venus is also home to strange volcanic features not found on any other planet. Lava oozing onto the surface creates formations known as pancake domes. There are also volcanic domes known as arachnoids, which are surrounded by spiderweb-like patterns of fractures and ridges, and ticks, in which landslides have carved out ridges that look like insect legs sticking out. Other volcanoes on Venus that have lava flows resembling a flower's petals extending outward are called anemonae.

Venus also has hundreds of giant circular volcanic features called coronae, which are surrounded by a ring of ridges and fractures. Some have central mounds, and some have craterlike depressions inside.

About 65 percent of Venus's dry, dusty, rocky surface is covered by flat or rolling plains, 27 percent is covered by lowlands, and 8 percent by highlands. Wrinkle ridges, formed by the wrinkling or buckling of the planet's crust, are found on the plains.

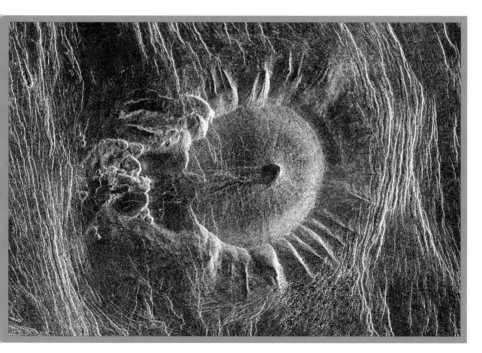

▲ The volcanic formation known as a tick, named for the tiny insect it resembles, is clearly shown in this photograph taken northeast of Alpha Regio.

Fractures in the planet's crust known as rift valleys occur when the crust pulls apart or is stretched. There are also highland regions and tall mountains. In Venus's northern hemisphere, the Lakshmi Plateau is larger and higher than the Tibetan Plateau on Earth. In the equatorial region, there are several canyons nearly two miles (about three kilometers) deep, more than one hundred miles (approximately one hundred sixty kilometers) wide, and hundreds of miles long.

Venus has fewer than a thousand impact craters. These craters form when meteors hit a planet's surface. There are no small craters such as those seen on the Moon. Small meteors are burned up by Venus's dense atmosphere before reaching the surface.

Although Venus no longer seems like a goddess of love, it is the only planet in our solar system named after a goddess. So astronomers named most surface features of the Venusian landscape after famous women in history and goddesses of various cultures. Detailed maps of Venus include names such as Mona Lisa, the famous subject of Leonardo da Vinci's painting; Cleopatra, the queen of Egypt in the first century B.C.; Sacajawea, the American Indian who served as a guide for the Lewis and Clark expedition; Emily Dickinson, the nineteenth-century American poet; and Ozza Mons, a Persian goddess.

Chapter 3 ▶

When a Day Is Longer Than a Year

Venus's mean, or average, distance from the Sun is 67 million miles (108 million kilometers). The planet completes its revolution around the Sun in about 225 Earth days. This is not surprising, since it has a shorter distance to travel than Earth. Earth, at a distance of about 93 million miles (150 million kilometers) from the Sun, takes 365 days to circle the Sun.

But there is something very peculiar about the rotation of Earth's twin planet. Earth, of course, rotates on its axis in 24 hours—one Earth day. And Earth completes 365 rotations in one Earth year. You might guess that Venus would have a similar relation between its orbital period and its rotational period. But you would be wrong. It takes Venus an incredibly slow 243 Earth days to rotate once on its axis. So one day on Venus is actually longer than one Venus year!

There is another unusual aspect to Venus's rotation. Unlike Earth and all the other planets except Uranus, Venus's rotation is retrograde, or "backward," moving counterclockwise rather than clockwise. In the unlikely event that you were ever able to spend time on the surface of Venus, a day would seem to last forever. Assuming you could see the Sun through the thick cloud cover, it would rise in the west instead of the east. According to one scientist, "You would have to wait about 61 Earth days for the Sun to reach high noon. It would finally set in the east after 121.5 Earth days."[1]

The slowness of Venus's rotation may be why the planet has no magnetic field. Although Venus is believed to have a core that is mostly iron, the planet rotates too slowly to generate enough electrical current to create the field. Venus's gravitational field is about 91 percent that of Earth's, meaning that a person who weighs 100 pounds (45 kilograms) on Earth would weigh only 91 pounds (41 kilograms) on Venus.

Venus's Orbit

When Galileo Galilei observed Venus through his telescope in 1610, he noticed that the planet went through a cycle of shape

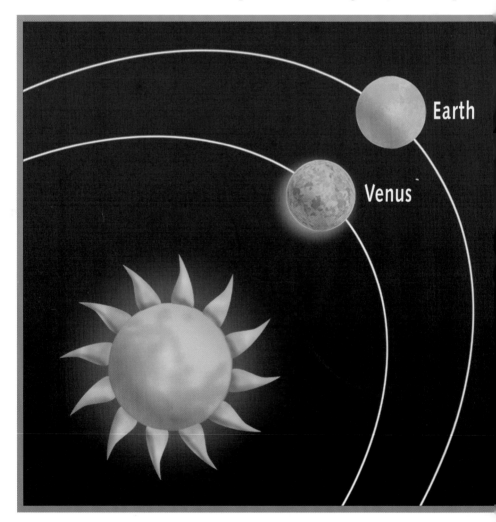

Earth

Venus

Venus is invisible to us when it passes between Earth and the Sun because its sunlit side is away from Earth.

http://www.vt-2004.org/photos/images/vt-photo-01-miwi.jpg - Microsoft Internet Explorer

File   Edit   View   Favorites   Tools   Help

Address http://www.vt-2004.org/photos/images/vt-photo-01-miwi.jpg   Go

Done   Internet

This photograph of the June 8, 2004, transit of Venus was taken in London, England. Seen in the beginning phase of the transit, Venus appears as a dark spot on the Sun's surface.

changes. Venus has phases like the Moon, waxing and waning from crescent to half to three-quarter, or "gibbous," to full and back again. Each cycle includes one complete evening appearance of Venus, one morning appearance, and two disappearances. As Venus travels along its orbit, it sometimes aligns with Earth and the Sun in such a way that it vanishes. Such disappearances last an average of eight days.

When Venus passes between Earth and the Sun, Venus is invisible to us because its non-sunlit side is turned toward us. Venus travels with the Sun through Earth's daytime sky. As Venus reappears to one side of the Sun, it becomes the morning star. Each day it rises earlier than the Sun. When Venus becomes visible three hours before sunrise, it has reached its maximum elongation, or distance, from the Sun as seen from Earth. This is when Venus is its brightest. Now Venus reverses course, moving closer to the Sun and rising closer to sunrise with each passing day. Finally, Venus disappears again, this time moving behind the Sun. When Venus reappears again, it can be seen after sunset and becomes the evening star, once again at its brightest.

When Venus passes exactly between Earth and the Sun, a transit, or alignment of Venus, Earth, and the Sun, occurs. Because Venus's orbit is slightly tilted from Earth's orbit by 3.5 degrees, transits are the rarest of planetary alignments. There have been only six seen since the telescope was invented, and the most recent was on June 8, 2004. During a transit, which lasts about five and a half hours, the dark outline of Venus can be seen as a black disk passing across the bright Sun. But to view this rare event, people are strongly advised to use a telescope that has a solar filter on the large end, because direct viewing of the Sun, even for just a few seconds, can cause serious damage to one's eyes and even blindness.

The Horned Planet

Although Galileo was the first person to observe the phases of Venus through a telescope, he was not the first person to see the planet's crescent phase. People with exceptionally good eyesight are able to make out Venus's crescent phase without using a telescope or binoculars. In ancient times, people who observed Venus's crescent shape believed the planet had horns. Legends often refer to the "horns" of Venus. Pliny the Elder, a first-century A.D. Roman naturalist, represents Venus as a human figure with two horns. The Assyrian Venus was pictured bearing a staff tipped with a crescent.[2] And on some Maya glyphs, pictorial writing on stone that recorded significant events and people, Venus is also shown with horns.

Chapter 4 ▶

The Runaway Greenhouse Effect

Referring to Venus's thick, poisonous atmosphere, the astronomer Carl Sagan wrote that "Venus is a kind of planet-wide catastrophe."[1] Sagan and many other scientists wondered why Venus is so hot. They reasoned that the constant cloud cover should have kept the planet's surface cool. The clouds prevent most of the Sun's heat (thermal radiation in the form of sunlight) from reaching Venus's surface, and the radiation is reflected back into space. But the relatively small amount of radiation reaching Venus's surface apparently was enough to turn Venus into a scalding inferno.

Sagan believed that Venus's high surface temperature was caused by a process known as the greenhouse effect. The theory of the greenhouse effect was first proposed in the 1940s by German-American scientist Rupert Wildt.[2] He compared the clouds of Venus to the glass roof and walls of a greenhouse. The

glass allows sunlight in to warm the plants, which then give off heat energy, but the glass also traps the heat inside so

An artist's conception of the surface of Venus depicts the kind of landscape one might find in science fiction. But Venus is in fact a fiery hot world of deadly gases.

that it cannot escape. The trapped heat results in the greenhouse getting even warmer. In a similar way, the carbon dioxide clouds of Venus allow the Sun's heat to penetrate Venus's surface but they do not allow all the heat to escape. But what would happen if this warming process were to spin out of control? This is what appears to have happened on Venus.

Too Much of a Good Thing

A greenhouse effect is not necessarily a bad thing for a planet. Earth has its own greenhouse effect, caused by carbon dioxide and water vapor. Life on our planet would not be possible without it. The global temperature of Earth would be below the freezing point of water (32°F; 0°C) if not for the greenhouse effect. The small amount of carbon dioxide in the atmosphere traps just the right amount of heat necessary to sustain life as we know it. But on Venus, the greenhouse effect proved to be too much of a good thing for the planet. The result was a runaway greenhouse effect.

Many scientists believe that at one time in the distant past, during the early days of the solar system, Venus may have had large bodies of water, perhaps even oceans like those on Earth. Both Venus and Earth began with atmospheres that contained carbon dioxide, nitrogen, and water vapor. On Earth, however, the carbon dioxide became dissolved in water and then was stored in carbonate rocks such as limestone. This may have happened on Venus also. As time went by, the Sun grew hotter and gave off more energy. This caused Venus to grow warmer. And because Venus is closer to the Sun than Earth is, there was more warming on Venus than on Earth. If the carbon dioxide locked in Earth's rocks were released now, Earth's atmosphere would be like Venus's!

As evaporation increased, water vapor entered the atmosphere. Water vapor and carbon dioxide are both powerful greenhouse gases. As Venus grew even warmer, more water boiled away, adding fuel to the fire. The high percentage of carbon dioxide in Venus's thick atmosphere trapped almost all of the Sun's heat,

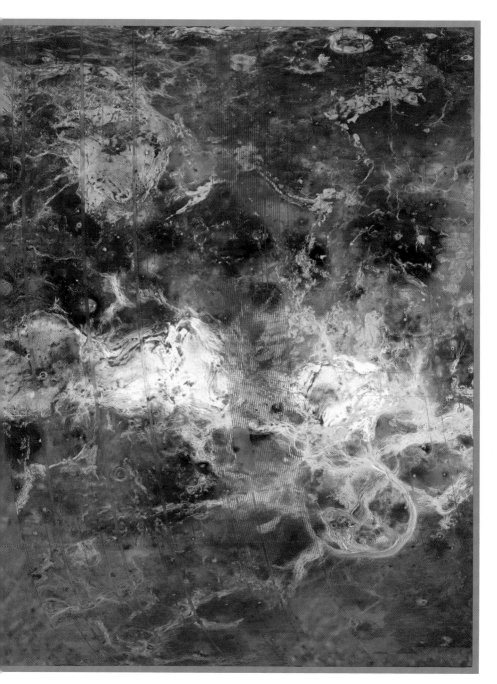

The eastern half of Venus is shown in this map of Venus's surface. The simulated colors in this NASA photograph are based on earlier color images recorded by two Soviet Venera spacecraft.

allowing barely any of it to escape back into space. The slowness of Venus's rotation also contributed to the overheating of the atmosphere. Eventually, the temperature of Venus reached the boiling point of water—212°F (100°C). At that time the oceans boiled away, and the runaway warm-up continued.

Meanwhile, Back on Earth

On Earth, we continue to rely on the burning of fossil fuels such as oil or petroleum, natural gas, and coal for most of our energy needs. These products are called fossil fuels because they were formed millions of years ago from plant and animal remains. And we are burning fossil fuels at an increasing rate. The burning of fossil fuels increases the amount of carbon dioxide in the atmosphere and may also contribute to global warming. If the global

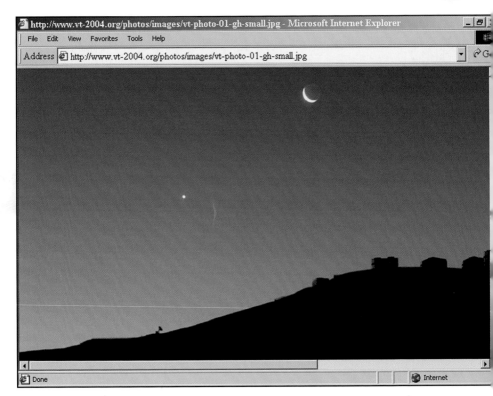

http://www.vt-2004.org/photos/images/vt-photo-01-gh-small.jpg - Microsoft Internet Explorer

File   Edit   View   Favorites   Tools   Help

Address http://www.vt-2004.org/photos/images/vt-photo-01-gh-small.jpg

Done   Internet

The evening star: a view of Venus and the Moon as seen from the Atacama Desert in Chile.

A global view of Venus displays its northern hemisphere. Venus's highest mountain, Maxwell Montes, appears as the bright part of the lower center of this photograph.

temperature of Earth rises by only a few degrees, more water vapor would stay in the atmosphere. The burning of fossil fuels also adds sulfuric acid to the atmosphere, creating acid rain.

According to one writer, "Venus is a tantalizing vision of an Earth that might have been—and a terrifying demonstration of what the Earth itself might have become had it been born closer to the Sun."[3] Many scientists are concerned about the effects of global warming on Earth. They hope to learn more about the nature and causes of Venus's runaway greenhouse effect to help prevent the same thing from happening on Earth.

Chapter 5 ▶

The Exploration of Venus

Most of our current knowledge of Earth's twin planet comes from unmanned space probes and landers that have sent back data from Venus. Until the mid-twentieth century, our understanding of Venus was based on several hundred years of telescopic observations and a combination of theorizing, educated guesswork, and active imagination. Then, in the late 1950s, radio astronomers

http://www.vt-2004.org/photos/images/vt-photo-01-pv.jpg - Microsoft Internet Explorer

File   Edit   View   Favorites   Tools   Help

Address   http://www.vt-2004.org/photos/images/vt-photo-01-pv.jpg

Done   Internet

▲ *For centuries, the only way that humans could see Venus was from Earth through a telescope. This image of Venus and the Pleiades, a star cluster in the constellation Taurus, comes from Livorno, Italy.*

△ Mariner 2, *launched in 1962, was the first successful interplanetary spacecraft and the first to record the temperature of Venus's atmosphere.*

detected radio-wave emissions coming from Venus. Those radio waves, which can only be produced through heat, suggested that the planet might be hot—much hotter than anyone had expected and much hotter than most scientists were prepared to accept at that time.

▷ Unmanned Exploration of Venus Begins

During the 1960s, the United States and the Soviet Union competed with each other in a space race. On April 12, 1961, Soviet cosmonaut Yuri Gagarin became the first human being to venture into space when he orbited Earth in a flight that lasted under two

Mariner 5, *launched on June 14, 1967, made a flyby of Venus on October 19 of that year. It flew within 2,500 miles (4,000 kilometers) of the planet.*

hours. Near the end of the decade, in 1969, American astronauts Neil Armstrong and Buzz Aldrin became the first humans to walk on the Moon. But while most of the world's attention was focused on the amazing missions of brave astronauts and cosmonauts, impressive progress was also occurring in American and Soviet unmanned space programs. Both the United States and the Soviet Union launched spacecraft to Venus and more distant planets throughout the 1960s and the decades that followed.

American and Soviet Missions to Venus

Venus was an early goal in the superpower space competition. Launched in August 1962 by the National Aeronautics and Space Administration (NASA), the American *Mariner 2* spacecraft reached Venus in December of that year. It became the first unmanned spacecraft to fly by another planet and send back information (the flyby lasted only forty-two minutes). It flew within 21,600 miles (34,754 kilometers) of Venus and scanned the surface. The data it sent back to Earth confirmed what radio astronomers in the 1950s had reported—that Venus is very hot. But the data also showed that Venus is hotter than anyone had expected. *Mariner 2* reported an atmospheric temperature of 540°F (300°C) near the surface. *Mariner 2* also carried magnetometers, instruments that can detect metals and measure the intensity of magnetic fields. They showed that Venus lacks a magnetic field.

The Soviets were also launching space probes to find out more information about Venus. The *Venera* spacecraft were covered in armor to survive the temperature and atmosphere on Venus. In 1967, the Soviet *Venera 4* flyby mission included a space probe that entered the atmosphere of Venus and fell toward the surface. As it descended, it recorded that the atmosphere consists mainly of carbon dioxide. It also reported cloud temperatures ranging from 100°F (38°C) to 525°F (274°C). The *Venera 4* probe may have crashed on the surface of Venus but probably burned up before

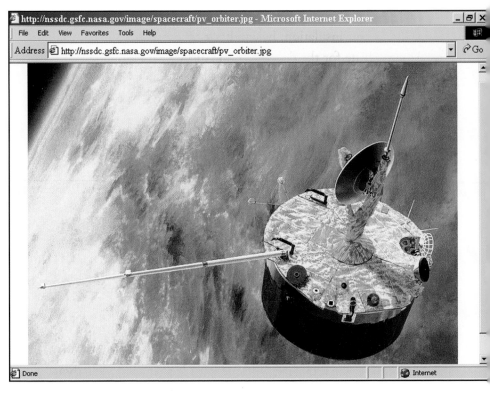

▲ The Pioneer Venus Orbiter, *whose mission lasted fourteen years, made the first detailed maps of Venus's surface.*

reaching the surface. At practically the same time that *Venera 4* entered Venus's atmosphere, the American *Mariner 5* spacecraft arrived at Venus for a flyby. *Mariner 5,* which flew as close as 2,544 miles (4,094 kilometers) to the planet, confirmed the high cloud and surface temperatures on Venus and lack of a magnetic field.

▷ First Glimpse of the Surface of Venus

The next challenge for Soviet and American scientists was to design a space probe that could make a soft landing on Venus. The lander would have to withstand the extreme heat during descent and crushing air pressure on the surface. It would also have to survive on the planet's surface long enough to send information back to Earth. The Soviet *Venera 7* spacecraft included a lander with extra-protective insulation, heavy shock absorbers for the landing, and a parachute for the descent to the surface.

On December 15, 1970, *Venera 7* became the first space probe to successfully land on another planet and send back data from the surface. *Venera 7* entered Venus's atmosphere and landed on the night side of the planet. It transmitted data for 35 minutes during its descent and another 23 minutes from the planet's surface. *Venera 7* reported a surface temperature of 880°F (471°C) and air pressure ninety-three times that on Earth's surface. Then on July 22, 1972, *Venera 8* landed on the day side of Venus. It transmitted data for 50 minutes. *Venera 8* reported high winds in the upper atmosphere and an absence of wind on the surface. It analyzed soil samples and found that uranium, thorium, and potassium were present on Venus. It also reported that only about 2 percent of the Sun's energy reaching Venus penetrated the clouds to the planet's surface.

In 1974, NASA's *Mariner 10* spacecraft, which was on its way to Mercury, made a close flyby of Venus. It sent back four thousand images of Venus's clouds, the first images of Venus produced from space. But the most exciting pictures came the following year. On October 22, 1975, the Soviet *Venera 9* probe landed in the northern hemisphere of Venus and sent back the first pictures from the surface of Venus. *Venera 9* continued to transmit black-and-white images of the surrounding landscape, showing a dark, rocky plain, for 53 minutes. Scientists identified the sharp-edged flat rocks as basalts, the result of volcanic activity. There was no indication that water had ever been present.

On October 25, 1975, *Venera 10* landed on Venus at a point 1,400 miles (2,253 kilometers) south of the area where *Venera 9* had landed. *Venera 10* sent back pictures of a different sort of landscape that included a more rounded type of rock. In 1978, *Venera 11* and *Venera 12* detected the presence of water vapor in Venus's atmosphere. This finding supported Carl Sagan's theory that Venus's runaway greenhouse was the result of a carbon-dioxide and water shield in the planet's atmosphere.[1] In 1982, the *Venera 13* and *Venera 14* landers drilled into Venus's surface and obtained samples of rocks, soil, sand, and dust. Chemical analyses of the samples showed them to be the result of volcanic action, similar to volcanic basalts on Earth. *Venera 13* transmitted the first color television images of Venus's surface, depicting a surface that has been described as a "rocky wasteland bathed in a sulphurous orange glow."[2]

Mapping the Surface of Venus

With each flyby or lander, scientists gained an enormous amount of new information about Venus. The next great leap forward in expanding our growing body of knowledge about Venus involved mapping the surface features of the planet.

In 1978, the United States launched the *Pioneer Venus Orbiter* spacecraft. It was supposed to orbit Venus for two years, but it performed well beyond anyone's expectations and continued to map the planet for fourteen years. It used an instrument known as a radar altimeter to make the first detailed maps of the surface of Venus, revealing the planet's mountains, plains, and valleys. It also released four probes into Venus's atmosphere. The *Pioneer* probes discovered that a thin layer of sulphuric acid particles in the upper atmosphere gives the clouds their yellowish color. *Pioneer* also detected flashes of lightning below the clouds.

In 1983, the Soviets launched *Venera 15* and *Venera 16,* which orbited Venus and used radar to map at least 25 percent of the planet's surface. Many of Venus's surface features now known to us were observed for the first time by these spacecraft and were included in the high-quality images gained from these missions.

In May 1989, the American *Magellan* spacecraft was launched from the space shuttle *Atlantis* and made two complete orbits around the Sun before arriving at Venus on August 10, 1990. Because *Magellan* orbited the planet's poles, it was able to view all latitudes of the planet. *Magellan's* radar-imaging system was able to map Venus's surface in great detail. By October 1994, *Magellan* had made fifteen thousand orbits of Venus and imaged 98 percent of the planet's surface. *Magellan* also completed a gravity field map of 95 percent of Venus.

Currently, there are at least two space missions planned that will reveal even more information about the planet. The purpose of NASA's *Messenger* mission, launched in 2004, is to study Mercury from orbit, but the spacecraft is scheduled to make two flybys of Venus in 2006 and 2007. And the *Venus Express* mission

△ The Mercury Surface, Space Environment, Geochemistry and Ranging mission, or Messenger, was launched in 2004. Designed to study the planet Mercury, it will also make three flybys of Venus.

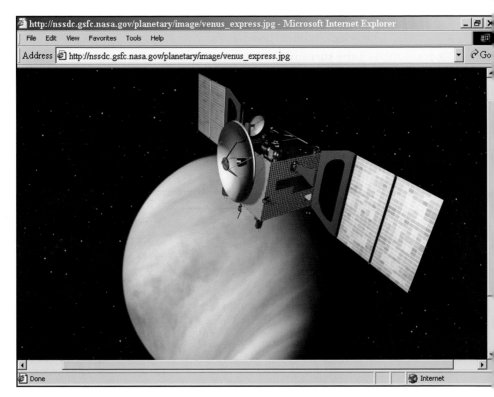

http://nssdc.gsfc.nasa.gov/planetary/image/venus_express.jpg - Microsoft Internet Explorer

File   Edit   View   Favorites   Tools   Help

Address 🔄 http://nssdc.gsfc.nasa.gov/planetary/image/venus_express.jpg   ▼ 𝒫 Go

Done   🌐 Internet

🔺 *In the fall of 2005, the European Space Agency will launch Venus Express, a mission to study the atmosphere and environment of Venus. This voyage to Venus will last for 153 days.*

of the European Space Agency is set to launch in November 2005 from Kazakhstan, a former Soviet republic. Its goal is to study the atmosphere of Venus.[3]

Scientists have already gathered a great deal of data from the many Venus space probes, orbiters, and landers that have transmitted data back to Earth. Some of Venus's mysteries have been revealed, but many more remain. Scientists now know that our mysterious twin planet is so unlike Earth that it seems strange to even hear it still referred to as a "twin." Yet, for all we now know about the poisonous conditions on the planet, Venus remains an object of beauty in the skies of Earth, as humans continue to admire the brightly shining morning and evening stars.

anemonae—Volcanoes whose lava flows spread out, like flower petals, toward the surrounding plains. (An anemone is also a type of flower.)

arachnoids—Volcanic domes surrounded by fractures and ridges that form a pattern resembling a spider web. (*Arachnids* refers to the class to which spiders belong.)

basalts—Dark rocks formed from volcanic activity.

geocentric theory—A theory that placed Earth at the center of the universe.

greenhouse effect—The warming of a planet through heat trapped in the planet's atmosphere.

heliocentric theory—A theory that places the Sun at the center of the solar system.

lava—Hot melted rock that pours from a volcano or a fissure, or crack, in a planet's surface.

magnetic field—A part of space near a magnetic body or a current-carrying body in which the magnetic forces can be detected.

magnetometer—An instrument used to measure magnetic fields.

satellite—A body in space, such as a moon, that orbits another larger body.

ticks—Volcanoes whose sides have ridges that jut out, like the legs of an insect.

ultraviolet rays—Invisible rays of light from the Sun that lie beyond the violet end of the spectrum.

Chapter 1. Earth's Twin Planet

1. Ian Ridpath and Wil Tirion, *Stars and Planets* (Princeton, N.J.: Princeton University Press, 2001), p. 346.

2. Patrick Moore, *Venus* (London, England: Cassell Illustrated, 2002), pp. 28–29.

3. Ibid., p. 42.

Chapter 2. Beneath the Clouds of Venus

1. Patrick Moore, *Venus* (London, England: Cassell Illustrated, 2002), p. 156.

2. Carl Sagan, *Cosmos* (New York: Random House, 1980), p. 97.

Chapter 3. When a Day Is Longer Than a Year

1. Thomas R Watters, *Planets: A Smithsonian Guide* (New York: Macmillan, 1995), p. 60.

2. Patrick Moore, *Venus* (London, England: Cassell Illustrated, 2002), p. 38.

Chapter 4. The Runaway Greenhouse Effect

1. Carl Sagan, *Cosmos* (New York: Random House, 1980), p. 97.

2. Editors of Time-Life Books, *The Near Planets* (Alexandria, Va.: Time-Life Books, 1989), p. 83.

3. Ian Ridpath and Wil Tirion, *Stars and Planets* (Princeton, N.J.: Princeton University Press, 2001), p. 346.

Chapter 5. The Exploration of Venus

1. Editors of Time-Life Books, *The Near Planets* (Alexandria, Va.: Time-Life Books, 1989), p. 89.

2. Ian Ridpath and Wil Tirion, *Stars and Planets* (Princeton, N.J.: Princeton University Press, 2001), p. 346.

3. NASA, National Space Science Data Center, "NSSDC Master Catalog: Spacecraft: Venus Express," n.d., <http://nssdc.gsfc.nasa.gov/database/MasterCatalog?sc=VENUS-EXP> (May 27, 2004).

Asimov, Isaac, with revisions and updating by Richard Hantula. *Venus.* Milwaukee: Gareth Stevens, 2002.

Challoner, Jack. *The Atlas of Space.* Brookfield, Conn.: Copper Beech Books, 2001.

Cole, Michael D. *Venus, the Second Planet.* Berkeley Heights, N.J.: Enslow Publishers, Inc., 2001.

Farndon, John. *Planets and Their Moons.* Brookfield, Conn.: Copper Beech Books, 2001.

Fimmel, Richard O., Lawrence Colin, and Eric Burgess. *Pioneer Venus: A Planet Unveiled.* NASA, Ames Research Center, 1995.

Fradin, Dennis Brindell. *The Planet Hunters: The Search for Other Worlds.* New York: Margaret K. McElderry Books, 1997.

Grinspoon, David Harry. *Venus Revealed: A New Look Below the Clouds of Our Mysterious Twin Planet.* Reading, Mass.: Addison-Wesley Publishing Company, Inc., 1997.

Henbest, Nigel. *A Guided Tour of Our Solar System Through the Eyes of America's Space Probes.* New York: Viking, 1992.

Ride, Sally, and Tam O'Shaughnessy. *Exploring Our Solar System.* New York: Crown Publishers, 2002.

Spangenburg, Ray, and Kit Moser. *Venus.* New York: Franklin Watts, 2001.

Stone, Tanya Lee. *Venus.* Tarrytown, N.Y.: Benchmark Books, 2003.

Stott, Carole, and Clint Twist. *1001 Facts About Space.* New York: Dorling Kindersley, 2002.